FARMHOUSE CHRISTMAS

FARMHOUSE CHRISTMAS

Anne Walton

Illustrated by Henry Brewis

Bridge Studios
Northumberland
1993

First published in Great Britain in 1993

by Bridge Studios,
Kirklands,
The Old Vicarage,
Scremerston,
Berwick-upon-Tweed
TD15 2RB

Tel: 0289 302658/330274

ISBN 1 872010 41 5

Printed by How & Blackhall
77 Marygate
Berwick-upon-Tweed
TD15 1BB
Tel/Fax: 0289 307553

CONTENTS

Without Pat who seems always to be around when I need her I doubt if this book would have seen the light of day. To my publishers, Keith and Lynne, for their ceaseless encouragement, a thousand thank-yous. And not forgetting dear Henry Brewis for his perfect drawings and of course Michael, my long-suffering husband!

INTRODUCTION

For me Christmas is best conjured up by smells. Just a whiff of cloves or cinnamon is enough to set me thinking of mince pies or mulled wine. A hint of orange puts me in mind of the fruit we always found tucked in the toes of our Christmas stockings when I was a child.

I grew up with my sisters in a large rambling farmhouse and every year at Christmas time the house was filled with love and laughter and, of course, food. We all had to help prepare gigantic servings of vegetables, there was the roast turkey and goose, dozens of mince pies, the huge round Christmas pudding brought flaming to the table and our favourites, the nuts and sweets and other treats.

The house was filled with greenery brought in by Dad from the woods and we always went to choose a tree with him which he cut down and we all carried home. That was my favourite time, when the tree was standing bare for us girls to decorate and turn into something out of a fairytale.

Of course at that age I didn't realise just how much hard work and planning went into making our magical Christmases possible. I do now, and I hope this book will give you some ideas and hints for a relatively stress-free time.

I think the important thing is to plan ahead — I make lists, lists and more lists! Whatever you can cook ahead and either freeze or store until you need it is invaluable. Only don't forget about it.

There are recipes in this book for basic festive fare, and there are also ideas for quick, easy meals to rustle up in a hurry. And remember, people love to receive home-made gifts, hence our section for making gifts. You can't start too soon with preserves, fruit in rum, pot-pourri and lavender bags which can all be made well before Christmas.

If you've read *Farmhouse Cooking*, then you will know that I've used imperial measurements throughout. I've done the same this time but I have included a conversion table on page 8 for the modern-minded!

And finally, most recipes serve four unless stated otherwise. Good cooking and Merry Christmas.

Anne Walton

CONVERSION TABLES

Liquid Capacity:

pts	*fl oz*	*ml*
¼	5	150
½	10	300
¾	15	425
1	20	600
1½	30	900
2	40	1200

1 teaspoon = 5 ml
1 dessertspoon = 10 ml
1 tablespoon = 15 ml

Weight:

oz	*g*	*oz*	*g*
1	25	9	250
2	50	10	275
3	75	11	300
4	115	12	335
5	150	13	375
6	175	14	400
7	200	15	425
8 (½ lb)	225	16 (1 lb)	450

Oven Temperatures:

To convert Celsius to Fahrenheit, multiply Celsius by 9, divide by 5 and add 32.
To convert Fahrenheit to Celsius: Fahrenheit $-32 \times 5 \div 9 = C$ (the reverse).

Oven Temperature Chart:

Celsius	*Fahrenheit*	*Gas Mark*	*Description*
130	250	½	Very cool
140	275	1	Very cool
150	300	2	Cool
160	325	3	Warm
180	350	4	Moderate
190	375	5	Fairly hot
200	400	6	Hot
220	425	7	Hot
230	450	8	Very Hot
240	475	9	Very hot

Soups, Starters and Nibbles

PARSLEY SOUP

Serves 6 — can be served hot or chilled.

a good handful fresh parsley
knob butter
1 medium onion
1 lb potatoes
2 pints chicken stock
2-3 tablespoons single cream
salt and freshly milled pepper

Parsley must be very fresh to retain flavour — it is added at the very end of the recipe and hardly cooked at all.

Melt butter in saucepan and add peeled and finely chopped onion. Fry gently for a moment or two to soften onion. Add peeled and cut up potatoes. Stir in stock and bring to the boil.
Cover with a lid and simmer gently for about 20 minutes or until potatoes are quite soft. Thoroughly wash parsley, pick off and discard stems and add to pan. Bring back to the boil and draw off heat. Run the vegetables and liquid through a blender goblet. Season to taste. Reheat or leave until cold and, before serving, stir in the cream.

SPINACH SOUP

1 lb spinach
knob butter
1 pint milk, infused with bay leaf and slice of onion
1¼ oz butter
1¼ oz flour
1 pint chicken stock
salt and pepper
a touch of nutmeg

Wash the spinach leaves in plenty of cold water and pull away from any coarse mid ribs. Drain well. Soften gently in the knob of butter over a low heat for 6-8 minutes. Make a white sauce with the milk, flour and butter and stir into spinach. Heat together for 5 minutes. Purée in a blender and thin to required consistency with chicken stock. Season to taste and reheat to serve. You can swirl in a little cream for a special occasion.

BIRNENSUPPE — PEAR SOUP

2 lb firm dessert pears, peeled, cored and diced
1 pint water
½ teaspoon aniseed
small piece cinnamon
3 oz sugar
2 oz seedless raisins
5 fl oz medium sweet sherry

Put the pears into a medium-sized pan and cover with water. Add the aniseed and cinnamon and gently poach the pears over low heat for about 40 minutes, or until tender. Place a strainer over a large bowl and force the softened pears through it with the back of a wooden spoon. Add sugar to taste.

Chill the soup in the fridge for 3 hours. Put the raisins in a medium-sized bowl and cover them with the sherry. When the soup has chilled, stir in the raisins and liquid and serve in small chilled bowls.

CARROT AND CORIANDER SOUP

1½ lb carrots
1 trimmed leek
knob of butter and a little oil
2 teaspoons ground coriander
1 tablespoon plain flour
2 pints chicken stock
salt and pepper
1 or 2 bay leaves

Clean the leeks and slice thinly. Dice the carrot (I sometimes pop the carrots in the Magimix and shred).

Heat the butter and oil and add the vegetables, cover and cook gently. (If liked add a little crushed garlic.) Soften the vegetables but do not colour. Stir in the ground coriander and flour and cook for about a minute before adding the stock.

Bring to the boil, season, add bay leaves, cover and simmer until all ingredients are cooked. Remove bay leaves.

Cool and then pop in blender. Put a little milk (or some single cream or even a small carton of natural yoghurt) into the blender jug to rinse it out. Check seasoning. Re-heat but do not boil.

CREAM OF CELERY SOUP

2 heads of celery, scrubbed and chopped (I add the leaves)
1 large onion, sliced
1 oz butter and a little oil
2 oz flour
1½-2 pints of chicken stock
blade of mace
a squeeze of lemon juice
celery salt and freshly ground pepper
a few carrots (use any leftover)

Melt the butter and oil, add the onion and then the celery, cook gently for about 5 minutes. Stir in the flour and cook for a few minutes. Gradually add the stock. Add the mace, lemon juice, celery salt (go carefully, it can be adjusted later) and pepper.
Bring to the boil cover and simmer for approximately 20 minutes or until tender. Take out the mace.
Purée in a blender (I usually put through a sieve as well in case the celery is at all stringy). Again I rinse out the blender jug with about ½ pint of milk or more depending upon thickness of soup. Adjust seasoning.

FRENCH ONION SOUP

2 oz butter plus a little oil
2 lb onions sliced
2½-3 pints brown stock
salt and pepper
4 oz Gruyere cheese, grated
6-8 thin slices of toasted French bread

Melt the butter and oil and add a sprinkling of sugar, fry the onions slowly until brown and soft.
Stir in the stock, bring to the boil and simmer with a lid on for 30-40 minutes. Season.
Pour into bowls (must be flameproof).
Sprinkle the cheese on the slices of toasted bread and put a piece on the top of each bowl of soup.
Put under a hot grill (or if an Aga in the top oven) until the cheese melts.

SPICED SALMON

1½ lb salmon tail, filleted
1½ tablespoons sea salt
2 teaspoons brown sugar
1 teaspoon cumin seeds
1 teaspoon coriander seeds
6 cardamom seeds
1 teaspoon black peppercorns
1 tablespoon brandy or gin

Crush the spices and peppercorns in a mortar or with the back of a wooden spoon. Mix with the rest of the ingredients (not the salmon). Spread some of the mixture in a shallow dish and lay one salmon fillet in it skin side down. Spread more mixture on top and place other fillet (skin side up) on top. Top with remaining mixture. Cover with cling film with a weight on top — tins of beans will do! Put in the fridge for up to 5 days. Use as you would smoked salmon.

Pomanders *are deliciously scented dried oranges studded with cloves and rolled in spices. You need small oranges or tangerines, several ounces of cloves — buy them loose, orris root powder, cinnamon and mixed spice. Push cloves into the oranges — the children love this job — if the skins are too tough, make small holes with a skewer. When your orange is covered with cloves put in a paper bag with the spices. Shake gently to make sure the orange is covered and then dry in a warm dark place for about three weeks. You can cheat by drying them on the top of an Aga or even in the bottom oven! Tie decorative ribbon round and use to hang on the tree or to give as presents — to hang in wardrobes or drawers.*

MELON IN GINGER WINE

Prepare in the morning and leave in the fridge covered with cling film for about 8 hours.

Cut a large ripe melon into small cubes and put into bowl. Pour over about 6 tablespoons of ginger wine. Put in fridge. Take out of fridge half an hour before serving. Put into individual dishes with a twist of orange and lemon slices.

AVOCADO AND CRAB

Flake white crabmeat and mix with some chopped chervil. Arrange sliced avocado around crabmeat on a plate and top crabmeat with a little soured cream, sprinkled with a touch of paprika. (If American caviar available sprinkle on top of cream.)

GAME PÂTÉ

1 lb belly pork
1 lb rabbit meat
½ lb pig's liver
1½ lb Roseden sausage meat
1 large onion, chopped
2-3 tablespoons sherry
chopped parsley, sage and a few mixed herbs
10 pieces of fat streaky bacon (may need more)
salt and pepper

Cut rabbit into small pieces. Put pork, liver, sausage meat and onion through mincer. Mix everything together and season well.
Line a loaf tin or a terrine with the bacon rashers. Put in the mixture and fold the bacon edges over the top. Cover with foil and place in a roasting tin with enough water to come half way up the sides of the tin.
Cook at Gas 3/325°F/160°C for about 3 hours. Cool in the tin.
Can be made 2 or 3 days before required, but when turned out of tin wrap in foil and refrigerate.

KIPPER PÂTÉ

(Popular, but do make sure to buy kipper fillets; it is time consuming to make sure all the bones are out.)

Skin 8 oz raw fillets and marinate in 4 tablespoons dry white wine for at least 12 hours. Purée in a food processor or blender, seasoning with freshly ground black pepper and 6 oz almost-melted butter. Put into ramekins, garnish with a half slice of lemon and a piece of parsley. Serve with toast.

SMOKED TROUT PÂTÉ

(Again time-consuming when it comes to taking out the bones, but well worth the effort.)

2 smoked trout
4 oz melted butter
squeeze of lemon juice
salt and pepper
grated rind of an orange

Put (hopefully) boneless and skinned smoked trout into food processor or blender, add lemon juice and orange rind, seasoning (check later so do not add too much at this stage). (I occasionally add a dessertspoon of horseradish sauce.) Add melted butter. A little of the juice of the orange can also be added. Put into ramekins. Garnish with half a twisted slice each of orange and lemon.

COD ROE PÂTÉ

tin of cod roe (I usually use smoked)
1 tablespoon white breadcrumbs
1 clove of garlic
juice of ½ lemon
freshly ground black pepper and salt (check when adding salt)
2-3 oz melted butter

Put all ingredients in blender, except butter, add when others are blended. Put into ramekins and garnish with halved cucumber and lemon slices. (I sometimes add chopped parsley to mixture.)

POTTED BEEF

1 lb of best stewing steak (Roseden's is good!)
5 fl oz stock
a sprinkling of mace (a clove if liked — not everyone likes the flavour!)
salt and pepper

Cut meat into small pieces, put in a casserole with stock and seasoning. Cover and cook Gas 4/350°F/180°C for 2½-3 hours until tender. Drain the stock off but retain. Place the meat in a blender and blend until smooth. Add 1 oz melted butter and add enough of the stock to moisten it. Put into ramekins and cover with the remainder of the melted butter. Ideal served with toast (or good for sandwiches with any salad ingredients preferred).

CHICKEN LIVER PÂTÉ WITH A DIFFERENCE

Since I discovered those jars of green peppercorns in brine I've been tempted to put them in everything! Seriously though, they do make a difference to a chicken liver pâté.

8 oz chicken livers
2½ oz butter
1 medium onion, chopped
2 oz rindless streaky bacon, cut into small pieces
1 crushed clove of garlic
½ teaspoon marjoram
2 teaspoons green peppercorns in brine, drained
2 teaspoons lemon juice
salt and pepper

Heat 1 oz of butter in a frying pan and cook bacon and onion until just beginning to brown. Raise heat slightly and add chicken livers and garlic, herbs and seasoning. Cook, turning from time to time until livers are brown on the outside but slightly pink inside. Cool for a few minutes and then whizz in a food processor with the remaining ingredients. Season to taste and put into small dishes and cover with foil. You could cover the surface of the pâté with a layer of clarified butter and decorate with more peppercorns and a bay leaf, particularly if you intend giving the pâté in a decorative dish as an edible Christmas gift. The pâté can be frozen, so you could make it in advance.

SMOKED SALMON PAÎE

You don't need whole smoked salmon slices for this pâté, just use the trimmings, they are often cheaper.

1 lb smoked salmon pieces
4 oz softened butter
8 tablespoons double cream
juice of a lemon or 4 teaspoonsful
freshly ground black pepper

Put all ingredients except pepper into a blender or food processor and whizz for a few seconds. Scrape down the sides and whizz for a few more seconds. Don't over-process. Season with black pepper to taste. Store in small dishes in fridge.

SALMON PÂTÉ

Serves 6

2 cans (7½ oz) pink salmon
¼ pint mayonnaise
¼ pint double cream
1 lemon, grated rind and juice
10 green stuffed olives
½ oz gelatine
¼ pint water
1 chicken stock cube
salt and pepper

Remove skin and bones from salmon and place in a food processor with the lemon rind, juice, mayonnaise, cream and salt and pepper to taste. Also add the olives and half the water and whizz until smooth. Put gelatine and stock cube and remaining water in a small basin and stand in a pan of hot water. Stir until gelatine dissolves and add to the other mixture. Whizz until smooth. Put into a small loaf tin and chill. When ready to serve turn out of tin and garnish with extra olives and parsley. Serve in slices with Melba toast, or just plain farmhouse toast!

Handy hint

Heat a lemon in hot water before squeezing out the juice and you should get almost double the amount of juice.

CHEESE STRAWS

8 oz self-raising flour
3 oz margarine
4 oz grated cheese
1 beaten egg
1 tablespoon milk
pinch of salt

Sprinkle salt into flour and rub in margarine. Add other ingredients to make a stiff dough. Roll out thinly and cut into even sized fingers. Prick with a fork and place on a greased baking tray. Bake 15-20 minutes at Gas 3-4/325-350°F/160-180°C.

Nuts always go down well at Christmas, but why buy expensive flavoured nuts when you can easily 'flavour' your own. Here are a couple of recipes that, once you've tried, you'll want to do time and time again.

ROASTED ALMONDS

Whole blanched almonds are ideal for this recipe but are quite pricey. It's better and cheaper to buy them with the skins on and blanch them yourself. Simply soak in a cup of very hot water for a few minutes and then pop off the skins.
All you need to do with these nuts is toss them in salt and place in a heavy oiled frying pan. Cook on top of the stove or in a fairly hot oven, but keep an eye on them and turn them frequently. They're ready when they are golden brown.

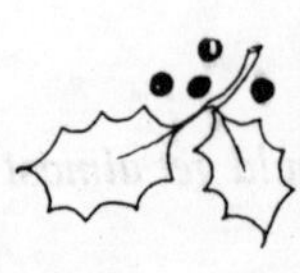

***Pine cones** are readily available if you live in the country and will last for years and years. I like them plain, tied on to artificial garlands with thin ribbon, but you can spray them with gold or silver spray paint if you like.*

SPICY PEANUTS

10 oz salted peanuts
1 oz melted butter
splash of soy sauce
dash of Tabasco sauce (a small dash, more like a few drops!)

Mix all ingredients together and tip on to Swiss roll tins. Bake at Gas 2/300°F/150°C for 15-20 minutes, turning the nuts once or twice during this time.
You can also use this recipe for cashew nuts, but the peanuts are less expensive so you get more for your money!

SPICED WALNUTS

8 oz walnut halves
2 tablespoons oil
1 tablespoon Worcestershire sauce
¼ teaspoon dried chillies
½ teaspoon celery seed
1 clove garlic
1 teaspoon dried mixed herbs
2 teaspoons sea salt

Heat oil in a pan and add all ingredients except the nuts. Mix well then add the nuts and cook over a gentle heat stirring frequently for 15 minutes. Put on a baking sheet and roast at Gas 4/350°F/185°C for 5 minutes until crisp. Cool on plate with paper towel on. Store in airtight jars until required.

The following versatile mixtures can be used to top small cocktail biscuits, oatcakes, vol-au-vents, small baked pastry tartlets or even small squares of toast and for hungry souls, sandwiches. You can make them in advance, refrigerate in covered containers and assemble your savouries at the last minute.

CHEESE FILLING

6 oz finely grated Edam cheese
2 eggs, hard-boiled and sieved
3 tablespoons mayonnaise
pinch dry mustard
pinch paprika
1 tablespoon chopped fresh parsley
salt and pepper

Mix all ingredients in a bowl until combined. Season to taste. Pipe onto biscuits or pastry cases or toast. Garnish with sprig of parsley, gherkin fans and small pieces of pimento.

CHEESE AND PRAWN FILLING

This is simply a mixture of cheese cut into small dice, and peeled prawns bound together with seafood dressing or mayonnaise. Use as before and garnish with a small twist of lemon secured with a cocktail stick.

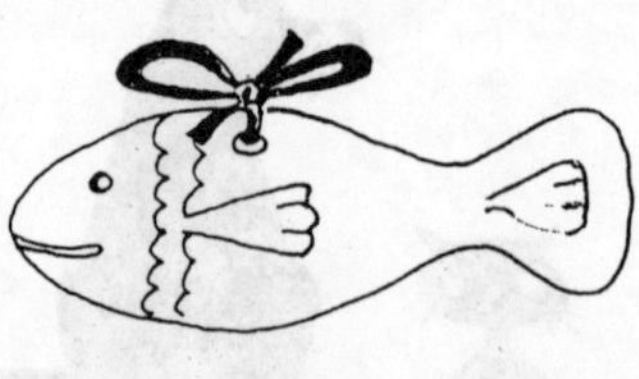

HAWAIIAN FILLING

4 tablespoons mayonnaise
4 chopped pineapple rings
4 oz finely grated Edam cheese
small green pepper, cored, de-seeded and finely chopped
4 slices lean ham, finely diced
pinch Cayenne pepper
dash Tabasco sauce
grated rind of half a lemon
1 teaspoon lemon juice
salt and pepper

Mix all ingredients together thoroughly, season to taste and use as before. Garnish with spring onion curls or very thinly cut onion rings.

CHEESE AND MUSHROOM FILLING

1 oz butter
1 oz plain flour
½ pint milk
salt
Cayenne pepper
4-6 oz grated Cheddar cheese
4 oz mushrooms, chopped and lightly fried

Make white sauce from butter, flour and milk, season to taste and add cheese and mushrooms. Stir until cheese has melted. Leave to cool and use as before.

***Salt dough decorations** can keep the children occupied while you are busy baking. Make the dough from one cup of salt to two cups of flour and a little oil. Add water a little at a time and knead to a stiff dough. Roll out to ¼ inch thick and cut shapes using cutters — stars, trees, gingerbread men shapes, crescent moon (use a plain round scone cutter to cut this shape). Make a small hole at the top of each shape, brush with egg white to glaze and bake in a slow oven until hard. When cool tie ribbon through and hang. They can be painted and varnished if wished.*

PHILLY ONION SPREAD

6 oz Philadelphia cheese
2 tablespoons milk or cream
1 tablespoon lemon juice
1 teaspoon finely grated onion
dash of paprika
1 teaspoon anchovy essence (if liked)

Cream cheese until smooth. Add lemon juice to milk or cream and gradually add to cheese. Blend well, working in onion, anchovy essence and paprika.

GARLIC STOTTIES

To have with soup or cold meats.

1 stotty between two people
3 oz softened butter
1 clove of garlic, crushed
salt to taste

Beat garlic into butter adding extra salt if necessary. Cut stotties in half so you have two pizza-like portions. Spread one portion with the garlic butter and sandwich together again. Wrap in foil and bake in a hot oven for about 20 minutes. Unwrap carefully, cut into wedges and serve.
A variation on this theme is to add a level teaspoonful of dried mixed herbs or even fresh herbs if they are available.

The Main Course

Christmas is such a special time that almost any meal can be a celebration, and that goes for anything you cook. It doesn't have to be the traditional turkey or goose, although turkey is marvellous if you're cooking for a crowd. If you are entertaining fewer people, what about duck or pheasant, or a crown roast of pork for a change. This section will give you recipes for the traditional basic fare as well as ideas for other meals throughout the festive season.

COOKING TIMES FOR YOUR CHRISTMAS MEAT

Roast Turkey

Gas Mark 3/325°F/160°C

Weight	*Hours*	
6 lb - 8 lb	2½-3½	
8 lb - 10 lb	3 -3½	
10 lb - 12 lb	3½-4	
12 lb - 14 lb	4 -4½	
14 lb - 16 lb	4½-5	
16 lb - 18 lb	5 -5½	usually slightly less
18 lb - 20 lb	5½-6	usually slightly less

To check if cooked — put a skewer deep into the thigh. A creamy pink colour is proof of being cooked. A red liquid means it is still underdone. Covering with foil (especially on the legs of a large bird) will prevent over browning. Remove towards the end of cooking. (It does slow down the cooking slightly.)

Roast Duck

Truss as for chicken except the wings are not drawn across the back. Prick all over with a fork or skewer and sprinkle with salt. Cook Gas 5/375°F/190°C for 20 minutes to the pound.

Roast Goose

Stuff and truss. Sprinkle with salt and if possible roast on a wire rack as goose is inclined to be fatty. Add a cooking apple to the tin, this will give the gravy a better flavour. Cook Gas 6/400°F/200°C for 15 minutes to the pound plus 15 minutes OR Gas 4/350°F/180°C for 25-30 minutes to the pound. (If covered with greaseproof paper, remove for the last 30 minutes.) Serve with gooseberry sauce for a change.

Roast Pheasant

Put a knob of butter inside and cover with strips of bacon. Cook at Gas 8/450°F/230°C for 10 minutes and reduce to Gas 6/400°F/200°C for a further 30 minutes or more according to size.

Roast Grouse
Season inside and out and cover with bacon. Cook at Gas 6/400°F/200°C for 30 minutes, basting occasionally. After 20 minutes remove the bacon, sprinkle on flour, baste and cook for another 10 minutes.

Roast Sirloin of Beef
For a piece on the bone weighing about 7 lb roast at Gas 7/425°F/220°C for 15 minutes per pound plus 20 minutes extra or 20 minutes per pound if preferred well done.

With your Christmas 'bird' you'll want to serve all the usual trimmings — bread sauce, chipolatas (Roseden's of course), cranberry sauce, bacon rolls and the stuffings. For a variety of vegetables see the next chapter.

BREAD SAUCE

1 pint milk
6 oz fresh breadcrumbs, preferably from an unsliced loaf
1 large onion
1 oz butter
cloves — as many as you like
dash of cream
salt and pepper

Peel the onion and stick cloves into it — the number you use is a matter of taste, but at least half a dozen. Simmer the onion in the milk for 15 minutes. Remove onion and pour milk over the breadcrumbs. Return to pan, add seasoning and butter and cook gently, stirring, for about 5 minutes. Stir in cream and serve. You can freeze this easily. To use, simply thaw and heat gently, adding a knob more butter and a dash of cream.

GOOSEBERRY SAUCE

1 lb gooseberries
brown sugar
1 oz ground almonds
knob butter
little orange rind
pinch cinnamon

Cook the gooseberries, blend in a food processor and sieve. While still hot, add brown sugar to taste, orange rind and cinnamon. Add ground almonds to thicken and a knob of butter. Serve warm with goose.

FRESH CRANBERRY SAUCE

½ lb fresh cranberries
2½ fl oz water
4-6 oz sugar

Place cranberries in water. Bring to the boil, cover and simmer until the cranberries pop and soften — roughly 7 minutes. Stir in sugar and some grated orange rind.

***Evergreen garlands** look good draped over a fireplace (make sure they are secure) or around a staircase. It takes ages to make them from scratch using only evergreen material so I cheat and tie sprigs of holly, ivy and conifers to plain green artificial ones (readily available in chain stores). I tie ribbon bows at intervals and/or pine cones.*

APRICOT STUFFING FOR GOOSE

4 oz dried apricots
4 oz seedless raisins
3 oz melted butter
10 oz white breadcrumbs
1 level teaspoon salt
1 green pepper, de-seeded and finely chopped

Snip apricots into small pieces and put with the raisins into a small saucepan. Cover with water, bring to the boil and then drain. Mix with breadcrumbs, salt and green pepper. Stir in melted butter with a fork. Use to stuff the body cavity of your goose.

SISTER SHEILA'S STUFFING

8 oz Roseden sausage meat
4 oz minced lean ham
6 oz breadcrumbs
4 oz suet
2-3 eggs
2 tablespoons chopped parsley
1 teaspoon chopped lemon thyme
nutmeg
salt and pepper

Mix all dry ingredients together, add beaten eggs and mix well. Season to taste with salt, pepper and nutmeg. Use to stuff turkey or chicken.

Handy hint

When cooking flans in an earthenware dish put a baking tray in the oven to get hot. Put the flan case on to the hot tray and this will help the pastry base to cook.

Handy hint

To refresh a stale loaf — wrap in foil and place in a hot oven for about 10 minutes but remember to cool in the foil.

SAUSAGE AND CHESTNUT STUFFING

1½ lb Roseden pork sausagemeat
1 lb chestnuts ready prepared or tinned
2 oz cashew nuts (optional)
1 oz butter
1 medium to large onion finely chopped
1 small clove garlic finely chopped
½ teaspoon mixed dried herbs
salt and freshly ground black pepper

Mix sausagemeat and chestnuts (puréed or whole) in a basin. Melt butter in a saucepan and cook onions and garlic gently until soft. Allow to cool and add to the sausagemeat and chestnuts. Stir in remaining ingredients and season to taste with salt and freshly ground black pepper. Mix thoroughly, best with the hands, though messy! You can freeze this until needed so it can be made well in advance of the day itself. Simply put into a polythene bag, label and freeze. When required, thaw and use for stuffing the turkey.

CHESTNUT AND APPLE STUFFING

1 tin natural chestnuts (1 lb 5 oz)
1 lb Roseden pork sausagemeat
1 lb cooking apples, peeled, cored and chopped small
1 medium onion finely chopped
1 egg beaten
salt and freshly ground black pepper

Drain the chestnuts and mash with a fork. Mix with other ingredients and season to taste. Bind together with the beaten egg. Use in the usual way.

PARSLEY STUFFING

8 oz breadcrumbs
4 oz margarine
1 egg
chopped parsley — about 2 handfuls

Mix all the ingredients together — with the hands again if you like! Bake in a moderate oven in an ovenproof dish for about 20 minutes.

PRESSED TONGUE

1 salted ox tongue (ask your butcher for this)
8 peppercorns
1 medium onion, peeled and studded with 4 cloves
1 sliced carrot
1 bayleaf

Wash the tongue and soak for 24 hours or less if it is not highly salted. Put into a saucepan, cover with cold water and bring to the boil. Remove any scum from the top. Add remaining ingredients and simmer until tender — ½ hour per pound weight. When cooked plunge briefly into cold water. Ease off the skin while still hot and remove any small bones. Return to cooking liquid to cool. When cold remove from the liquid, which you should keep, and curve into a deep cake tin lined with foil. The cooking liquid should set when cold. If it doesn't, reduce it by boiling fast or add a little gelatine. Cover the meat with the cooled, strained liquid. Press with a heavily weighted plate if you don't have a tongue press. Chill.

SPECIAL GLAZE FOR HAM

4 tablespoons honey or syrup
1 lemon — zest and 4 teaspoons juice
2 teaspoons Worcestershire sauce

Cook ham and remove skin. Mix above ingredients together and spread over ham. Put back into the oven for the last half hour of cooking time.

Recycle wrapping paper*, or buy plain paper and decorate with potato prints.*

SUGAR-GLAZED GAMMON

3½ lb middle-cut gammon
1 onion peeled and stuck with a few cloves
1 bayleaf
1 pint dry cider
2 dozen cloves
½ teaspoon black peppercorns
2 tablespoons dark brown sugar
1 tablespoon made-up English mustard

Place gammon joint in a saucepan and cover with cold water, bring to the boil and discard water. To the pan add the bayleaf, peppercorns and onion and pour in ¾ pint of the cider with enough water to cover. Bring to the boil and simmer gently for 1 hour. Remove gammon and allow to cool a little. Remove the skin with a sharp knife. Preheat the oven to Gas 6/400°F/200°C. Now score the fat of the gammon diagonally, first in one direction and then the other so that you end up with a diamond pattern. Insert a clove into each diamond and spread mustard all over the joint. Then press the brown sugar all over – it is easiest to do this with your hands. Put the joint into a roasting tin with the remaining ¼ pint of cider in the bottom. Bake for 45 minutes, basting now and then with the cider and juices.

GINGERED GAMMON

gammon joint
4 oz preserved ginger in syrup
1 teaspoon orange juice

Cook gammon in the normal way as for the previous recipe. Cool slightly and remove the skin. Place in roasting tin. Slice ginger and place pieces on top of the joint. Mix the syrup and orange juice and pour over. Return to a moderate oven for 15 minutes basting frequently.

Jars of home made preserves *can be given the festive touch with circles of Christmassy cloth edged with pinking shears, tied round their tops with ribbon.*

DUCK WITH PINEAPPLE

Allow 1 duckling for 2 people

Cook duckling. When cooked, keep warm. Add a finely chopped cooked onion to the juices in the tin with a tablespoon of clear honey, a teaspoon of ground ginger and some chopped pineapple pieces. Add about half a pint of stock (use a chicken stock cube if not making stock with the giblets), a little lemon juice. Thicken with a little plain flour. Serve with the duckling and sprinkle with parsley.

BRAISED PIGEONS

3 sticks of celery
1 carrot, diced
1 medium onion, finely chopped
4 pigeons (one per person)
30 fl oz stock
bouquet garni
3 oz diced bacon
salt and freshly ground black pepper

Put the vegetables and bacon into a casserole dish and put the pigeons on top (whole or in portions, possibly better portioned). Add the stock and bouquet garni, season with salt and black pepper. Cover and cook for about 1 hour until the pigeons are tender. Uncover and cook for about 30 minutes, reducing the stock and browning the pigeons. The stock should be reduced but if necessary thicken with plain flour. Served garnished with watercress.

Cinnamon bundles *are easy and attractive to use to decorate your tree as well as giving a lovely spicy scent. Simply tie two or three cinnamon sticks with bright ribbon, tartan ribbon is good, and hang to decorate a tree or garland.*

PIGEONS WITH A CREAM SAUCE

4 pigeons
3 oz butter
5 fl oz stock
redcurrant jelly
7½ fl oz double cream
dash of brandy

Wash the pigeons. Fry in the butter until brown. Put in a casserole with the butter and juices from the pan, breast side down. Add the stock and some freshly ground pepper. Cover and cook at Gas 3/325°F/160°C for 1½ to 2 hours until tender. Remove pigeons and keep warm. Reduce the juices to half. Add redcurrant jelly and cream. Ignite brandy and stir into the sauce.

CROWN ROAST PORK

(Ask the butcher to chine two loins as he would for a crown roast of lamb.) Shape and tie together for form a crown, bones on the outside. Place on a rack in roasting tin. Season with salt and pepper. Wrap bones in foil and make a ball of foil and press into the middle to keep cavity open. Roast uncovered at Gas 3/325°F/160°C for 2 hours (this is for a weight of approximately 7 lb). Baste occasionally. Remove from the oven and remove foil from the centre. Fill with a sage and onion stuffing or one of your own choice. Cover the stuffing with a piece of foil. Roast for a further hour or until the meat is tender. Place on carving dish and allow to rest for 10 minutes. Remove foil and cover bone ends with paper frills or cherry tomatoes. Slice between ribs. Should serve 8-10.

An alternative stuffing is one using apricots and pine nuts.

APRICOT AND PINE NUT STUFFING

6 oz dried apricots
5 fl oz orange juice
2 oz butter
1 medium onion finely chopped
4 oz celery finely chopped
breadcrumbs

1 Bramley apple peeled and chopped
3 oz pine nuts (if not available chop some almonds)
salt, freshly ground pepper — to taste
½ teaspoon sage

Simmer apricots and orange juice until fruit is soft. Cook onion and celery in melted butter. Place all ingredients in a large bowl and mix together. Use to stuff crown roast or can be put in a greased casserole and baked at Gas 3/325°F/160°C and served separately.

PORK WITH JUNIPER BERRIES

4 lb boned loin of pork
thinly sliced clove of garlic (use more according to taste)
12-14 juniper berries, crushed
10 fl oz stock
5 fl oz dry white wine

Insert garlic slices in small incisions all over the pork and sprinkle with crushed juniper berries. Roll up and secure with string. Put the meat in a roasting tin (preferably on a rack) and roast for 30-35 minutes per pound. Remove meat from tin to serving dish and keep warm.
Pour off fat from tin and add stock and wine. Bring to the boil and reduce slightly.

Handy hint

If sour cream is not available, add a little lemon juice to fresh cream.

Handy hint

When frying in butter, add 1 tablespoon of oil to every 2 oz of butter to stop burning too quickly.

Finally, don't forget fish at this time of year. Salmon is usually readily available, makes a change from meat and of course will do for any vegetarians in the family.

DARNE OF SALMON WITH WATERCRESS SAUCE

4-6 salmon steaks — cooked in court bouillon

Watercress Sauce

8 oz watercress
knob butter
5 oz crême fraiche
1 teaspoon white wine vinegar
salt and pepper

Whizz the watercress leaves in a food processor with the butter. Heat gently with the remaining ingredients. Season with salt and freshly ground black pepper and pour over salmon.

KEITH'S CREAMY SALMON STEAKS

Serves 2 people

1 thick salmon steak (2")
⅓ pint double cream
1 tablespoon grainy mustard
2 teaspoons lemon juice
1 tablespoon chopped dill leaves or 2 teaspoons dried dill
salt and pepper

Place salmon in an ovenproof dish. Mix remaining ingredients and season with salt and pepper. Pour over the fish. Cover with foil and bake in a moderate oven Gas 4/350°F/180°C for about 30 minutes. Serve hot or cold with the sauce poured over.

Vegetable Dishes

This is a selection of traditional and more unusual vegetable accompaniments. I am assuming that everyone knows how to roast a potato!

NUTTY SPROUTS

Brussels sprouts
1 oz flaked almonds
knob butter
finely grated rind and juice of ½ lemon
salt and pepper

Prepare the sprouts and steam or boil until tender. Meanwhile slightly brown the almonds in the butter in a small pan. Add the lemon rind and juice. Drain the sprouts well and pour over the lemon butter mixture. Season to taste.

RED CABBAGE WITH CHESTNUTS

Red cabbage goes perfectly with all Christmas meats and is good tempered enough to stand reheating. If your menu is heavy on the chestnuts, that is if you've got chestnuts in the stuffing, then you can leave them out of this recipe and it will taste just as good.

1 medium sized red cabbage
1 medium onion sliced
1 large cooking apple peeled, cored and sliced
2 oz seedless raisins
¼ pint cheap red wine
1 tablespoon cider vinegar
1 tin peeled chestnuts
2 oz butter or bacon dripping
1 tablespoon soft brown sugar
¼ teaspoon powdered cloves
¼ teaspoon grated nutmeg
salt and ground black pepper

Shred the cabbage finely, discarding any outer leaves or white root. Cover with boiling water for a couple of minutes, then drain. Melt butter in a heavy casserole and fry onion until golden. Add remaining ingredients, except for the sugar and the chestnuts and add the cabbage and a good grating of black pepper and mix well. Cover tightly and simmer gently for about 1 hour. Turn from time to time. Stir in sugar and chestnuts, warm through and serve.

PARSNIPS

To roast — parboil halved parsnips for 5 minutes in salted water. Dry on kitchen paper and add to roasting tin for about an hour before the meat is cooked.

CARROTS 'N' NEEPS

I'm very fond of turnips, or bagies as we call them, but I like them diluted a bit with some carrots. Prepare equal quantities of carrots and turnip and cut into equal sized portions. Cook together in salted water until just tender. Mash roughly with a potato masher adding a good knob of butter, freshly ground black pepper and a grating of nutmeg.

CARROTS 'N' PARSNIPS

This is a variation on the previous dish. In place of the turnips use parsnips. Cook the carrots and parsnips in the same way, chop them roughly together and serve.

CARROTS GLAZED WITH BROWN SUGAR

1 lb carrots
knob of butter
2 tablespoons of brown sugar
juice of an orange

Prepare carrots and slice thinly. Cook as normal. Drain and add a knob of butter, sugar and orange juice. Heat gently until butter is melted and sugar dissolved. Simmer for about 5 minutes.

***Christmas stockings** are easily made from scraps of red cloth. Cut out stocking shapes from a double layer of material, stitch and cut round with pinking shears. Decorate tops with white fur fabric or cotton wool, add a hanging loop and hang. Make them in different sizes. Small ones could be used for home made sweets, suitably wrapped.*

CRISPY ONION RINGS

Cut required number of onion rings.
Have ready a dish for seasoned flour and one for milk.
Heat some fat in frying pan. Dip each onion ring into milk and then seasoned flour. Fry until cooked and serve. If preferred, deep fry.

BRAISED CELERY

celery cut in lengths of about 2″
knob of butter and olive oil
2-3 oz unsmoked bacon
1 carrot finely sliced
1 onion finely sliced
1 bay leaf
1 clove of garlic, sliced (optional)
½ pint beef stock
salt and pepper

Blanch celery for about 5 minutes. Put butter and olive oil into an ovenproof dish and place on medium heat. Add chopped bacon, carrot, onion, bay leaf and garlic (if used). When onion is transparent add stock, season and add celery. Cover and cook in a moderate oven for 40 minutes.

LEEKS

Wash 1 lb of leeks and cut into 2″ lengths. Put 5 fl oz stock into a pan, add a small knob of butter. Put on a medium heat and bring to the boil. Add the leeks, some chopped parsley (if liked), cover and cook for approximately 10 minutes until most of the liquid has evaporated.
I sometimes add a teaspoon of grainy mustard to the water before adding the leeks when serving them with pork.

Handy hint
Buy chicory as white as possible. If there are traces of green on the tips it will be bitter.

PEAS WITH PIMENTOS

1 lb packet of frozen peas
small tin of pimentos
1 small onion
good knob of butter
pinch of herbs
seasoning

Drain pimentos and chop finely. Chop onion finely. Sauté the pimentos and onion in the butter in a saucepan.
Cook the peas in another pan, drain and add to pimentos and onion. Sprinkle with herbs.
This can be prepared in advance and re-heated with a little extra butter if required.

APPLE AND ONION

To serve with pork sausages
1½ lb onions, thinly sliced
1½ lb apples, cored and thinly sliced (leave skins if thin)
4 tablespoons flour
3 tablespoons sugar
2 teaspoons salt
butter

Mix flour, sugar and salt and toss apples in mixture. In an ovenproof buttered oval dish, layer onions and apples alternately, finishing with onions. Dot with butter.
Cover with a piece of greaseproof paper and cook at Gas 4/350°F/180°C for 30 minutes or until tender. Uncover and brown slightly.
For a variation on this dish I substitute thinly sliced potatoes for the apples and add stock or cream, cooking in the same way.

Handy hint

Save celery tops (if not being used for soup) and dry in the oven. Rub to a powder and store in a glass jar. Use for soups and stews.

A CANADIAN RECIPE FOR A VEGETARIAN

1 bunch of fresh broccoli
1 cup of mayonnaise
1 can of cream of celery soup
6 eggs, well beaten
1 oz grated cheese
1 small onion, chopped very fine
salt and pepper

Cook broccoli and put in a greased casserole. Mix together other ingredients and pour over broccoli. Top with grated cheese for color, sorry, colour! Place casserole dish in pan of hot water and bake Gas 1-2/300°F/150°C until set in the middle — 1¼ hours.
This can very easily be made, refrigerated and re-heated successfully covering with foil.

WINTER VEGETABLE CASSEROLE

This is another recipe from Canada

1 cup onion rings
2 cups green beans
¾ cup of green pepper
1½ cups sliced carrots
2 cups tinned tomatoes
grated cheese
breadcrumbs
butter
salt and pepper

Mix all ingredients. Put in casserole and sprinkle with breadcrumbs and cheese (the recipe says Minute Tapioca — ugh!). Dot with butter and bake for 1½ hours. Sprinkle with Parmesan if liked.

For a welcoming front door *buy a simple green wreath and add your own trimmings — baubles, pine cones, ribbon.*

CHEESY COURGETTES

This is a more exotic dish to serve with your meat although it probably goes better with darker meats or game. It could also serve as a main course vegetarian dish.

2 large courgettes, washed and sliced thinly
1 small onion, finely chopped
1 tin plum tomatoes
1 clove garlic, crushed
1 tablespoon olive oil
2 oz Edam cheese, grated
¼ pint cream
1 teaspoon mixed herbs
salt and ground black pepper

Fry onions and garlic gently in olive oil in a heavy pan, add the tomatoes and mixed herbs and cook briefly breaking up the tomatoes. Cook gently for about 10 minutes. Lay the sliced courgettes over the tomato mixture and season with salt and black pepper, cover with a lid and simmer until the courgettes are tender, about 5 minutes. Meanwhile reduce the cream in a small pan until thick. Pour over the courgettes. Sprinkle grated cheese over and flash under the grill until brown. The advantage of this dish is that you can prepare it in advance and re-heat in the oven until brown.

COURGETTES WITH PASTA SHAPES

1½ lb courgettes
12 oz pasta, use the fancy shapes
1 large onion
1 clove garlic (if liked)
3 oz butter
salt and pepper
grated Parmesan (optional)

Slice and blanch the courgettes. Drain. Add the pasta to boiling water, stir until the water is boiling, simmer for approximately 12 minutes, until tender. Melt half the butter in a frying pan and fry onion until soft. (Add garlic if used.) Add the drained courgettes and seasoning, cover, cook for about 5 minutes.
Drain the pasta, add the courgettes and grated Parmesan (if used). Add the remaining butter.

DUCHESSE POTATOES

(Very useful as they can be prepared and frozen.)

Use leftover potatoes but I prefer to use freshly boiled potatoes and mash with butter, egg, a little salt and a touch of grated nutmeg. If necessary, sieve the potatoes then add the butter, etc.
Line a baking tray with non-stick paper. Fit an icing bag with large star nozzle and pipe pyramids on to the paper, the base of each 2 inches or slightly smaller.
Freeze uncovered. If baking tray not needed leave on this or if freezing for any length of time slide off tray into covered containers or polythene bags. When required, grease baking tray, put on potatoes and brush lightly with egg glaze. Put into a cold oven and cook Gas 6/400°F/200°C until heated and lightly browned.

A POTATO DISH

Make this ahead, cover and refrigerate.

Cook and mash 10 large potatoes. Add 10 fl oz sour cream, 2-3 oz butter, 1 packet of cream cheese and 2 teaspoons of grated onion. Season to taste. Put in oval ovenproof dish. Dot with butter. Cover and cook Gas 4/350°F/180°C for 30 minutes.

Desserts

Desserts are my downfall. From sticky gooey puddings to ice cream — I love them all. Here's a selection of the most calorific — who cares, it's Christmas!

AN EASY CHRISTMAS PUDDING

There are two good Christmas pudding recipes in *Farmhouse Cooking*, so here's an easy one. Don't forget, Christmas puddings are best made in advance and stored until you need them.

8 oz plain flour
½ teaspoon grated nutmeg
1 teaspoon cinnamon
4 oz soft brown sugar
8 oz chopped glacé cherries
2 large jars mincemeat
6-8 oz white breadcrumbs
grated rind of 1½ lemons
3 oz chopped almonds
5 eggs

Grease 2 two-pint pudding basins or use smaller depending on size required. Place a circle of greaseproof paper in the base of each one.
Sift the flour, cinnamon and nutmeg in a large bowl. Add the breadcrumbs, sugar, cherries, lemon rind and almonds. Mix and add the mincemeat and beaten eggs. Stir well. Cover with greased greaseproof paper and foil, securing firmly.
Steam for 4-5 hours. Remember to top up with hot water.
Store with greaseproof paper but use fresh foil to re-heat for about 2½ hours.

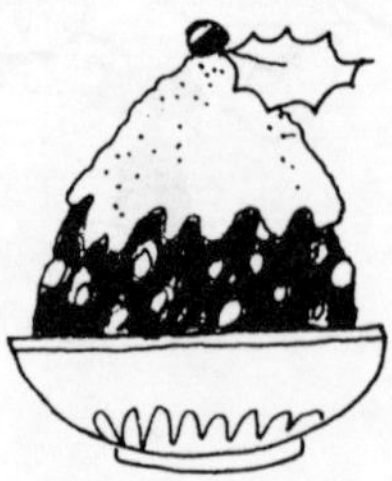

ALICE'S MOTHER'S PLUM PUDDING

1 small cup plain flour
1 large cup raisins
1 large cup currants
1 large cup breadcrumbs
1 large cup peeled, cored and chopped apples
1 large cup suet
1 large cup sugar
1 teaspoon mixed spice
2 teaspoons baking powder
1 egg
piece of lemon peel
¼ pint milk
1 glass rum or whisky (optional)

Mix all ingredients together and put into large greased basin. Cover top with greaseproof and a cloth tied round with string. Simmer for several hours.

MINCEMEAT

1 lb suet
1 lb currants
2 lb sultanas
2 lb cooking apples, peeled and cored
2 lb granulated sugar
4 oz mixed peel
2 oz chopped almonds
½ oz mixed spice
3 lemons, grated rind and juice
4 tablespoons brandy

Mince apples and sultanas and mix with all the other ingredients preferably by hand — you can mix more thoroughly and if making something like a fruit cake, the temperature of your hand melts the butter! Pot and cover in the normal way. Use mincemeat with either of the following pastry recipes. Make mince pies in advance of Christmas and freeze uncooked or cooked.

ROSE(DEN) CRUST PASTRY

6 oz flour
6 oz cornflour
5 oz block margarine
2 oz icing sugar
1 egg

Cream the margarine and icing sugar together. Sieve flour and cornflour together and mix with fat and sugar. Bind with a little beaten egg. (Save any left over egg to glaze.) Use as necessary and bake Gas 5/375°F/190°C, 12-15 minutes.

RICH PASTRY

6 oz self-raising flour
4 oz block margarine
2 oz caster sugar
2 oz ground almonds
grated rind of half a lemon
small egg yolk
a little milk

Rub fat into flour and stir in other dry ingredients. Bind mixture with the egg yolk and a little milk. Use as required. Cook Gas 6/400°F/200°C, 5-10 minutes.

MINCEMEAT FLAN WITH COINTREAU

Pastry Base
6 oz flour
3 oz butter
3 egg yolks
3 oz caster sugar
2-3 drops vanilla essence

Make pastry either by hand or in a food processor. Chill in fridge for an hour. Roll out and line a fluted flan tin (7½″ diameter). Bake blind for 10 minutes at Gas 5/375°F/190°C, then remove paper and baking beans and bake for a further 5-10 minutes. Cool.

Filling

1 lb mincemeat
2 oz ground almonds
2 lemons, grated rind only
2 oranges, grated rind only
6 oz seedless grapes, halved
2 tablespoons Cointreau
1 egg white
½ pint double cream

Mix mincemeat, almonds, half the grated rind, grapes and Cointreau together and spoon into the pastry case. Bake for 10 minutes at Gas 4/350°F/180°C. Cool. Whip the cream and remaining citrus rind. Whisk egg white and fold into cream. Spoon onto the mincemeat. Serve immediately.

CREAM CHEESE PASTRY

This pastry is delicious for fruit pies

9 oz cream cheese
12 oz softened butter
1½ lb plain flour

Blend cream cheese and butter. Gradually mix in flour until a dough is formed. Chill overnight (or at least an hour if needed the same day).

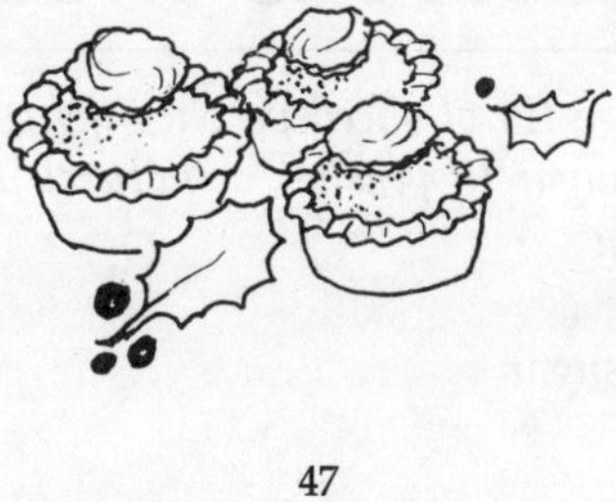

TOPPING FOR A CRUMBLE

6 oz flour
2 oz porridge oats (I sometimes vary by putting 1 oz coconut and 1 oz oats)
4 oz margarine
4 oz granulated sugar (I sometimes use demerara)

Mix flour and margarine to crumbs and add the rest of the ingredients. Use any fruit in the bottom of an ovenproof dish (don't forget to add sugar if fruit not cooked). Top with the above mixture. Bake Gas 5/375°F/190°C for 30 minutes.

SHERRY TRIFLE

5 trifle sponges
strawberry or raspberry jam
16 oz tin sliced peaches, reserve some of the syrup
3 tablespoons sherry
finely chopped blanched almonds and a few crushed ratafia biscuits
15 fl oz cooled pouring custard
½ pint double cream

Split the trifle sponges in half lengthwise, spread with jam and put together again. Break into pieces and arrange in a shallow dish (I prefer a glass dish). Drain the peaches, reserving some of the syrup. Arrange on top of the sponge. Reserve some slices for decoration.
Mix a little syrup with the sherry and pour over. Scatter chopped almonds and broken ratafias over top. Pour over custard.
Decorate with whipped cream, reserved peaches, a few cherries if liked and some toasted almonds. Chill.

PEACHES WITH SOFT BROWN SUGAR & CREAM

6 large peaches (buy a large tin of sliced peaches if fresh are not available)
3 tablespoons soft brown sugar (if peaches in natural juice, less if in syrup)
½ level teaspoon cinnamon
15 fl oz soured cream
6 level tablespoons caster sugar

Arrange the sliced peaches in ramekins. Mix the brown sugar with the cinnamon and sprinkle over the peaches. Spoon the soured cream over the peaches, sprinkle each with a tablespoon of caster sugar (it makes 6). Put under a very hot grill until sugar melts and caramelises. Chill before serving.

STUFFED PEACHES IN BRANDY

large tin of peach halves
2 oz ground almonds
2 tablespoons brandy

Drain the peaches and dry thoroughly. Boil the juice with a little of the brandy and allow to cool. Mix ground almonds with a little of the juice mixture and fill each peach. Add rest of brandy to the sauce and pour over the peaches.

BRANDY POTS WITH APPLES

3 lb Bramleys peeled and sliced finely
grated rind of at least one orange — about 3 teaspoons
5 fl oz orange juice
3 tablespoons brandy
6 teaspoons caster sugar possibly more according to taste
1 pinch of cinnamon
½ pint whipped cream

Mix the orange rind, juice and brandy. Pack the apple slices into 6 small soufflé dishes and sprinkle with caster sugar. Pour over the orange juice and brandy mix. Cover with buttered greaseproof. If possible put a small weight on each. Bake on a baking tray in a slow oven Mark 1-2/265°F/140°C for about 1½ hours. Decorate with whipped cream dusted with a little cinnamon.

A minute of thought is worth an hour of talk.

SNOWBALL PUDDING

(From a friend in Wales)

8 oz cream cheese
3 oz caster sugar
3 oz melted butter (preferably unsalted)
2 oz chopped hazelnuts
1 oz candied peel
2 oz glacé cherries
2 oz crystallised ginger
grated rind and juice of 2 oranges and 1 lemon
8 trifle sponges
½ oz gelatine dissolved in 2 tablespoons water (and juices)
5 fl oz double cream

Beat the cheese with sugar and melted butter. Stir in chopped nuts, candied peel, ginger, chopped cherries and orange and lemon rinds. Slice sponges across to give three slices to each sponge. Cover base of 2 pint pudding basin with slices (approximately 3). Spoon on a layer of cheese mixture then a layer of sponge until basin is full, ending with a layer of sponge.
Strain the juices (containing the gelatine) over the mixture in the basin, making sure it gets to the bottom of the basin by easing the mixture back with a spoon or knife. Put the basin in the fridge to set. When chilled, turn pudding on to a serving dish (dip briefly in hot water to loosen). Decorate with the whipped cream and a sprig of holly.

STICKY TOFFEE PUDDING

3 oz unsalted butter
3 eggs
15 fl oz water
9 oz self-raising flour
9 oz caster sugar
9 oz chopped dates
1½ teaspoons bicarbonate of soda
1½ teaspoons vanilla essence

Sauce
15 fl oz double cream
3 oz demerara sugar
1½ tablespoons black treacle

Cream butter and sugar until light and fluffy. Add eggs and beat well. Boil dates in the water for about 10 minutes until soft, add bicarbonate of soda. Mix the flour, dates and vanilla essence into butter mixture and pour into a greased 12″ × 8″ baking tray. Cook in oven for approximately 30-40 minutes until just firm to touch, Gas 4/350°F/180°C.
Boil cream, demerara and black treacle together. Pour over top of sponge until covered (there will be some left). Place under hot grill until it begins to bubble. Remove and cut into squares. Serve with remaining sauce.
This pudding can be made in advance and re-heated just before serving.
It can also be made in individual moulds.

QUEEN OF PUDDINGS

1 pint milk
5 oz breadcrumbs
2 eggs
1 oz butter
1 lemon
lemon flavouring
3½ oz sugar
jam

Boil the milk with some strips of lemon rind. Strain it over the breadcrumbs and cook them for a few minutes. Cool slightly, add the butter, 2 oz sugar and yolks of eggs.
Pour into a buttered pie dish. Bake in a moderate oven for about half an hour. Spread the jam over.
Whisk egg whites until stiff and add 1½ oz sugar. Pile on top of pudding and cook until crisp.

CABINET PUDDING

Serves 5

4 sponge cakes
ratafias
1 pint milk
3 eggs
almond or vanilla essence
1 oz sugar
1 oz glacé cherries
1 oz sultanas
1 oz peel
jam sauce

Well grease a mould and decorate with cherries. Cut sponge cakes into dice and put in mould in layers with chopped peel, sultanas and ratafias.
Boil the milk and pour on to the well-beaten eggs. Add the sugar and flavouring and pour into mould. Allow it to soak. Place a greased paper over and steam for 1 to 1½ hours.
Serve with jam sauce — put 2 tablespoons jam, 1 teaspoon lemon juice, 5 fl oz water in a pan and boil for 10 minutes. If necessary add a little colouring.

BREAD AND BUTTER PUDDING

This is strictly NOT nursery food so keep away from children!

8 oz pears, peeled, cored and sliced
1 cooking apple, peeled, cored and sliced
4 oz sultanas
2 oz blanched, chopped almonds
4 tablespoons whisky
grated rind of 1 lemon
2 oz brown sugar
5 slices bread, buttered and crusts removed
3 eggs
½ pint milk
¼ pint cream

Place fruit, nuts and lemon rind in a greased ovenproof dish and pour over the whisky. Cut bread into fingers and place buttered side up over the fruit. Warm the milk and cream and whisk in the eggs and 1 oz sugar. Strain this mixture over the bread and sprinkle remaining sugar over. Bake Gas 4/350°F/180°C for 30-40 minutes.

APRICOT MERINGUE PUDDING

large can apricot pie filling
2 eggs, separated
8 sponge fingers
8 tablespoons caster sugar
½ orange, grated rind and juice

Stir orange rind into pie filling and place in a soufflé dish. Whisk yolks and orange juice together and one by one dip the sponge fingers into the mixture. As each one softens arrange over the pie filling. Pour over any remaining mixture. Whisk egg whites until stiff, whisk in half the sugar and fold in the rest. Pile over the sponge fingers. Bake Gas 3/325°F/160°C for 20-30 minutes. Serve with cream.

MALVERN PUDDING

My son Peter has just married a lass from Malvern, so here's a delicious recipe for Malvern Pudding to make her feel at home.

1 lb cooking apples, peeled, cored and sliced
2½ oz butter
2 oz granulated sugar
2 oz demerara sugar
1 oz flour
¾ pint milk
1 egg
½ teaspoon cinnamon
1 lemon

Put 1 oz of butter in a saucepan and heat until melted. Add the apples and 1 oz of the granulated sugar. Cover and cook gently until soft, stirring occasionally. Remove from heat and stir in the grated rind of the lemon. Put in the bottom of a pie dish.
Make a sauce with 1 oz butter and the flour and milk and bring to the boil stirring all the time. Simmer for a couple of minutes, remove from the heat and stir in 1 oz granulated sugar and beat in the egg a little at a time. Cook for a further minute, stirring, then pour over the apple mixture. Mix the cinnamon and demerara sugar and sprinkle over the sauce. Dot with the remaining butter and grill until the sugar has caramelised.

PAVLOVA

3 egg whites
6 oz caster sugar
2 teaspoons cornflour
½ teaspoon vanilla essence
½ teaspoon vinegar

Whisk the egg whites until stiff. Add half the sugar and whisk again until the mixture forms peaks. Fold in the rest of the sugar, cornflour, vanilla and vinegar. Form a round on a baking sheet covered with baking parchment. Bake Gas ¼/225°F/110°C for 1½-2 hours. Cool and fill with whipped cream and fruit.

CHOCOLATE SUNDAE

4 oz good quality plain chocolate
1 oz butter
2 tablespoons milk
1½ teaspoons vanilla essence
vanilla ice cream
whipped cream
chopped nuts

Melt chocolate and butter and stir in milk and vanilla essence to make a chocolate sauce. Put scoops of ice cream into sundae glasses and pour over the chocolate sauce. Add whipped cream and sprinkle with chopped nuts to decorate.

SPEEDY SPECIAL DESSERT

Given a spare moment, make some sponge cakes and freeze. For a very quick, very impressive dessert, sandwich two defrosted cakes together with coffee ice cream and serve immediately. Use any other strong-flavoured ice cream.

QUICK TOPPINGS FOR ICE CREAM

These recipes are good standbys for desserts in a hurry and children love them. Make sure you've got some ice cream in the freezer though.

Chocolate Sauce

4 oz sugar
5 fl oz water
4 oz dark chocolate
1 oz butter

Melt all the ingredients gently in a small saucepan until just bubbling. Serve hot over ice cream.

Butterscotch Sauce

2 oz butter
2 oz soft light brown sugar
2 tablespoons golden syrup
2 oz chopped nuts

Melt butter in a heavy saucepan and add the sugar and syrup. Heat, stirring until sugar has melted. Boil for 1 minute. Stir in the chopped nuts and serve poured over ice cream.

BRANDY BUTTER

8 oz butter, unsalted is best
8 oz icing sugar, sieved
8 tablespoons double cream
6 tablespoons brandy
2 egg yolks
1 orange, grated rind only

Beat the butter and sugar together and add the cream and egg yolks a little at a time. Beat in the brandy and orange rind. Put into small pots and cover. This can be frozen (make it in advance; but don't forget about it) — or stored for up to a week in the fridge. Use as required, not just on the Christmas pudding or the mince pies but on hot fruits such as baked bananas or even fruit pies.

WHISKY BUTTER

4 oz butter
4 oz light soft brown sugar
¼ teaspoon mixed spice
1 orange, grated rind only
3 tablespoons whisky
1 teaspoon lemon juice

Beat the butter and sugar together. Add the rind and mixed spice. Beat in the whisky and lemon juice. Put into small bowls and cover. This can also be frozen, but it will keep for up to a week in the fridge.

Cakes and Biscuits

CHRISTMAS CAKE

11 oz butter
10 oz sugar
11 oz plain flour
4 oz cherries
4 oz ground almonds
1 lb currants
1 lb sultanas
6 eggs
4 tablespoons brandy

Beat the butter and sugar together until creamy. Add the eggs one at a time. Add flour a little at a time and lastly add the fruit. Bake for 3-4 hours in a moderate oven, Gas 3/325°F/160°C.
To prevent the cake from cooking too quickly I line my cake tin with 2 layers of newspaper — *The Farmer and Stockbreeder* is best! Then I put a lining of baking parchment before putting the cake mixture into the tin.
Alternatively, tie 4 layers of newspaper or brown paper round the outside of the tin with string.

CANADIAN WHITE FRUIT CAKE

½ lb caster sugar
2 eggs
4 oz butter
8 oz flour
1 level teaspoon baking powder
4 oz sultanas
4 oz mixed peel
4 oz Brazil nuts (make sure the nuts are fresh)
4 oz halved cherries
½ small teacup of milk
8 oz tin pineapple, drained and chopped (or use crushed)

Cream butter and sugar. Add beaten eggs and sifted flour with baking powder. Gradually stir in milk. Add remainder of ingredients. Bake in 7″ lined tin for 2½ hours in slow oven Gas 1-2/275-300°F/140-150°C.

BLACK FOREST GATEAU

3 large eggs
6 oz caster sugar
5 oz plain flour
1 oz cocoa
2 level teaspoons baking powder
2 tablespoons hot water

Filling

14 oz tin of black cherries
½ pint whipping cream
½ oz arrowroot
2 tablespoons liqueur
grated chocolate

Separate eggs and beat whites until stiff. Add yolks and caster sugar. Sieve in flour, cocoa and a pinch of salt. Add 2 tablespoons hot water. Bake in moderate oven about 40 minutes.
Cut in three. Whip cream. Put liqueur on bottom of sponge. Spread cream on top and add fruit. Put next sponge on and a little liqueur. Spread on cream and put on top sponge. Spread cream on top and around side. Sprinkle grated chocolate on top and around side. Pipe rosettes of cream around edge on top.

CRANBERRY CARROT CAKE

15 oz flour
10 oz brown sugar
1 teaspoon baking powder
1 teaspoon baking soda
½ teaspoon salt
½ teaspoon cinnamon
½ teaspoon grated nutmeg

Combine all these ingredients together in a bowl and add:

10 oz shredded carrot
10 oz coarsely chopped cranberries

Blend 2 eggs and 7 oz vegetable oil in a separate bowl, beating well. Add to the dry ingredients, beat until mixed. Put in greased 8″ square cake tin. Bake Gas 4/375°F/180°C for 40-45 minutes.
Ice with lemon flavoured icing.

SUPERIOR SWISS ROLL

1 oz cocoa
2½ oz sifted self-raising flour
3 eggs
4 oz caster sugar

Heat oven Gas 8/450°F/230°C. Bake sugar for 6 minutes. Break eggs on to the sugar and beat until it trebles itself. Add sieved flour and cocoa and pour into Swiss roll tin and bake for 6 minutes at the above temperature. Turn on to sugared paper and spread with butter icing and roll. This will not crack when rolled.

CHOCOLATE LOG

Make two Swiss rolls, or cheat and use bought ones if short of time!
Cover a cake board with icing sugar. Cut a small piece off one Swiss roll (this small piece not needed and can be put with some other slices to make candle decorations).
Make a good quantity of chocolate butter icing. Spread butter icing over both Swiss rolls. Put the larger one on the board and the smaller one at an angle against the other. Fork the butter icing to look like bark. Cover the ends with butter icing. Add suitable decorations, i.e. a robin, holly leaves, 'Merry Christmas'.
To make the candles, put a slice of Swiss roll on the board, put a milk flake in the centre, add a quartered cherry for the flame and drizzle some white butter icing down the side of the flake. If liked add four pieces of sliced peach around the base or any fruit preferred, mainly for colour. A pineapple ring could also be used.

GINGERBREAD

1 lb self-raising flour
8 oz butter
8 oz soft brown sugar
8 oz black treacle
8 oz golden syrup
2 eggs
1 tablespoon ground ginger
½ teaspoon allspice
pinch salt
small tub of plain yoghurt

Melt butter with the sugar and syrup and allow to cool. Sieve the flour and spices. Beat the eggs and mix with the yoghurt. Combine all ingredients together adding milk if necessary to make a fairly sloppy mixture. Pour into a fairly large square cake tin or roasting tin which has been lined with baking parchment. Bake Gas 2/300°F/150°C for just over 1 hour until firm. This cake will keep well in a tin, in fact it's better for keeping.

CHOCOLATE BISCUIT CAKE

8 oz plain chocolate (I like Bournville — it is a very rich dessert chocolate)
8 oz butter
2 eggs
1 tablespoon rum (tip the bottle a bit more if liked)
chopped walnuts and glacé cherries (use coloured cherries for a change)
2 dessertspoons light brown sugar (or use caster)
8 oz broken-up digestive biscuits — not crumbs

Butter a loose based 7″ cake tin. Melt chocolate in basin over boiling water or in a microwave. Melt butter.
Beat eggs and add sugar. Pour melted butter into egg mix and add chocolate — beat in. Fold in biscuits, walnuts, cherries and rum. Put in tin and refrigerate.

Handy hint

Grate some chocolate ready to put on a chocolate cake immediately it comes out of the oven OR use peppermint chocolate. If necessary return to the oven for a minute and when melted spread over with a palette knife.

SNOWMEN

4 oz margarine
4 oz caster sugar
4 oz self-raising flour
2 eggs

Place all the ingredients in a bowl and beat for two minutes, or use an electric mixer at slow speed. Place the mixture in two greased dariole moulds and bake at Gas 4/350°F/180°C until cooked.

For the next step you will need:

raspberry jam
desiccated coconut
6 white marshmallows
6 flat sandwich liquorice allsorts
3 liquorice pieces
a few drops red food colouring
icing sugar

Cover the baked shapes with jam and coat with the desiccated coconut. Make a little water icing and use to stick a marshmallow on top of each shape. Cut each liquorice piece in half and stick on to sandwich liquorice allsort with a little icing to make a hat. Stick on to top of marshmallow. Colour the remaining icing red and pipe markings for the face, buttons and a tie round his neck. In fact with a little imagination you can have a group of very different looking snowmen!

For a children's party, put each child's name on a snowman and use it as a place marker.

PARADISE FINGERS

shortcrust pastry to line a Swiss roll tin
4 oz butter
4 oz caster sugar
1 teacup sultanas
2 tablespoons ground rice
2 tablespoons chopped cherries
1 tablespoon chopped walnuts

1 tablespoon ground almonds
1 egg
vanilla essence
jam

Line the tin with pastry and spread with jam. Cream the butter and sugar, add the beaten egg and mix in the remaining ingredients. Smooth the filling over the pastry. Bake in a moderate oven for 35-40 minutes. Leave in the tin until cold. Sprinkle with icing sugar and cut into fingers.

DANISH MEDALS

Can also be used as a pastry.

8 oz flour
3½ oz icing sugar
4 oz butter
2 egg yolks

Work flour and butter to crumbs. Add sugar and egg yolks and mix well. Roll out very thinly and cut with medium-sized wine glass. Place on a greased baking sheet and bake in a moderate oven until golden brown.

Handy hints from Lucy

For cake making, in case (impossible?) you run out of eggs — two teaspoons of malt vinegar equals one egg. One cup of warm milk and one tablespoon of syrup equals three eggs.
(Need I add, being a farmer's wife, I haven't tested these!)

SNOWBALLS

2 oz caster sugar
2 oz margarine
3 oz desiccated coconut
3 oz porridge oats
3 tablespoons drinking chocolate
3 tablespoons condensed milk
marshmallows
extra desiccated coconut

In a small saucepan heat together the margarine, condensed milk, sugar and chocolate. Remove from the heat and stir in the coconut and the oats. Cut marshmallows in half and mould balls of the mixture with a half marshmallow in the centre of each one. Roll in extra desiccated coconut and leave to cool.

AUNTY ENA'S SHORTBREAD

8 oz butter
2 oz ground rice
10 oz plain flour
4 oz caster sugar
pinch of salt

Mix sugar, flour, ground rice and pinch of salt. Mix into butter. Bake in a moderate oven until slightly coloured and firm to the touch.

RICH CHOCOLATE SHORTBREAD

8 oz flour
6 oz butter
3 oz caster sugar
1 oz cocoa
1 tablespoon milk

Cream the butter and sugar until light and fluffy. Sieve the cocoa and flour and gradually mix into the butter and sugar mixture. Add a little milk if it is too dry. Roll out to desired thickness, I make mine just under an inch thick. Cut into fingers and prick with a fork. Bake Gas 5/375°F/190°C for 12 to 15 minutes until firm. Cool and sprinkle with icing sugar.

EDIBLE TREE COOKIES

4 oz flour
1 tablespoon golden syrup
1 tablespoon soft brown sugar
2 oz margarine
1 teaspoon black treacle
water
pinch each of cinnamon, ground ginger, nutmeg, mixed spice
pinch each of bicarbonate of soda, baking powder

Put syrup, sugar, treacle, water and spices in a small pan and heat gently, stirring from time to time until bubbling. Remove from heat and stir in margarine, bicarbonate of soda and baking powder. When the fat has melted add the syrup mixture to the sieved flour and mix until you get a soft dough. Roll out to ¼″ thick and cut out shapes — stars, trees, bells, etc., making a hole at the top of each one to put a ribbon through when cooked. Cook on a greased baking sheet Gas 4/350°F/180°C for about 10 minutes. They should be golden brown. When cool pipe with icing, thread fine ribbon through and hang on the tree.

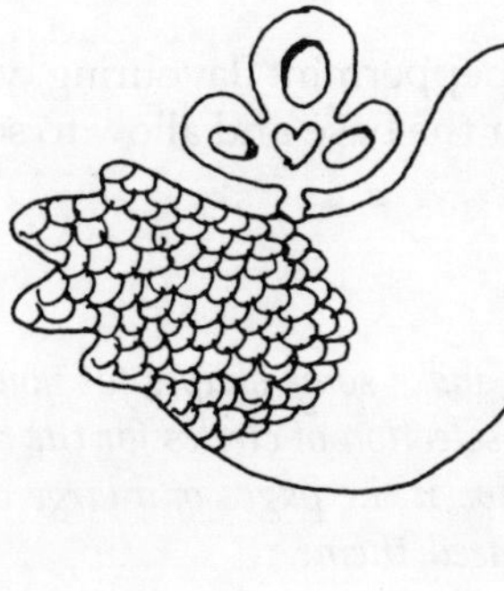

MERINGUES

For every egg white allow 2 oz caster sugar.
Old eggs make better meringues, not fresh eggs.

Whisk egg whites until very stiff. Whisk in half the sugar and fold in the rest with a metal spoon. Spoon on to baking parchment and bake in a very cool oven Gas ¼/225°F/110°C for at least 2 hours, or until they will just fit off the paper. Leave to cool. Store in an airtight tin for up to a month. These are again good to bake ahead and store. Sandwich together with cream for tea, serve with ice cream and fresh fruit for a dessert, serve with rum pot and cream poured over for an extra special pud!

PEPPERMINT SLICES

Base

4 oz margarine
1 cup self-raising flour
½ cup soft brown sugar
1 tablespoon cocoa
3 cups crushed cornflakes

Melt margarine and stir in remaining ingredients. Pour into a greased Swiss roll tin and bake Gas 4/350°F/180°C for 15-20 minutes.

Filling

8 oz icing sugar
½ teaspoon peppermint flavouring
water to mix
4 oz plain chocolate

Make up icing sugar and add peppermint flavouring, you can also add green colouring if liked. Spread over the base and allow to set. Cover with melted chocolate and cut into fingers.

Handy hint

When you've a minute to spare, make some shapes for your usual cake tins out of parchment or greaseproof, cut a selection of circles for the bases and long strips for the sides. Store flat — place between the pages of a large cook book and they'll be ready for use immediately you need them.

FRANGIPAN TARTLETS

6 oz short crust pastry to line tartlet tins or paper cases
4 oz margarine
4 oz caster sugar
1 large egg
4 oz ground almonds
1 oz plain flour
1 dessertspoon lemon juice
flaked almonds
glacé cherries
1 tablespoon warm apricot jam (Co-op apricot jam does not require sieving)

Cream margarine and sugar and beat in egg. Fold in ground almonds, flour and lemon juice. Put a teaspoon of mixture into each pastry case and sprinkle a few flaked almonds on top. Bake Gas 5/375°F/190°C.
While still warm brush with apricot jam and decorate with cherries.

ALMOND PASTE

4 oz icing sugar, sifted
4 oz caster sugar
8 oz ground almonds
1 teaspoon lemon juice
a little almond essence
beaten egg yolk to mix

Blend sugars and ground almonds together. Add lemon juice and a touch of almond essence. Add enough beaten egg to bind together. Turn on to a sugared board (caster and icing sugar mixed) and knead lightly until smooth. Some can be coloured to make holly leaves with berries or to make a Father Christmas (make a template with a piece of white card). Make stars or candles using food colouring to colour.

Handy hint

For an apricot glaze put the contents of a 1 pound jar of apricot jam with 4 tablespoons of water into a pan over a low heat. Stir until the jam softens. Sieve and return to the pan. Bring to the boil and boil until the glaze is a coating consistency. When cool return to jar ready for future use.

FONDANT ICING

¼ pint water
1 lb granulated sugar
1 oz glucose or a good pinch of cream of tartar

Use a strong, large heavy pan (large enough to stop the syrup boiling over). Put the water in the pan adding the sugar and allow to dissolve slowly (without stirring). When it is dissolved bring the syrup to the boil, add the glucose or cream of tartar and boil to 240°F. Pour into a heat resistant bowl and leave to cool until a skin forms on top. Beat until it thickens then work with a knife and finally knead with the hands until smooth. Colouring can be added. Can be used straight away or stored.
To use, put icing in a basin over hot water and heat to the consistency of thick cream. Can be diluted with sugar syrup/water. When using do not touch with a knife, or the gloss will be spoilt. For a large cake put on a wire rack with a plate below and pour over quickly.

***Ribbons** are a good, easy way to add the festive touch. Tie a wide red ribbon round your iced cake and finish with a bow. Tie tartan or red bows to your candlesticks and use red candles. You haven't a large enough table cloth? — use a plain white sheet with big red ribbon bows tied at the corners. Add red mats and napkins.*

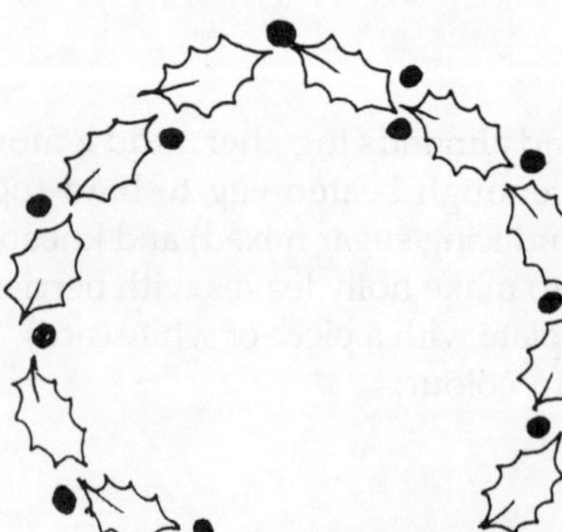

Leftovers, Suppers and Breakfasts

It's always a problem knowing what to do with the leftovers, but with a little imagination you can rustle up a variety of different dishes. There are plenty of ideas here for using up cooked meat and vegetables, as well as suggestions for supper dishes and interesting breakfast dishes.

COOKED CHICKEN IN CRANBERRY SAUCE

letftover chicken cut into pieces
6 oz cranberries
3 tablespoons sugar
9 tablespoons mayonnaise
1 tablespoon horseradish sauce
double cream

Cook the cranberries (if using fresh) with the sugar for 7 minutes. Cool. Combine the cranberry mixture with the horseradish and mayonnaise and a dash of cream. Put the chicken into a bowl with some lettuce as a base and mask with the cranberry mixture.

ROSEDEN CUTLETS

Enough for about 10 cutlets

leftover cold game, chicken or turkey
4 oz ham or tongue, chopped
2-3 mushrooms, chopped finely or minced
5 fl oz milk
1 oz butter
1 oz flour
yolk of 1 egg
½ small onion, grated
1 blade of mace
salt and cayenne pepper
egg and breadcrumbs

Boil the milk with the onion and mace, simmer and strain. Make a sauce with the butter, flour and flavoured milk. Add the egg yolk and re-heat but do not boil. Mix in the finely chopped meats, seasoning and mushrooms. Cool on a plate and form into tiny cutlets, using a little flour. Coat with egg and breadcrumbs. Fry in hot fat or oil.

Better to slip with the foot than with the tongue.

LYNNE'S GRANNY'S TURKEY SOUP

When you've finished with the turkey and there's a mere skeleton left, then the thing to do is make some soup which should keep you going until well into January.

Break up the carcase and put into the biggest pan you can find together with a large peeled onion, two peeled carrots, a couple of sticks of celery, a few peppercorns and 8 oz yellow split peas. Cover with water and bring to the boil, skim and simmer gently for 2 or 3 hours. If you have an Aga you can leave it overnight in the simmering oven.

The next thing to do is to allow it to cool slightly and then sieve all the ingredients into a clean pan, removing the bones. Use a wire sieve and a wooden spoon. Retain any pieces of turkey remaining on the bones to put in the soup, but everything else can go through the sieve. Don't be tempted to cheat and use the processor because it doesn't turn out the same! You should end up with a fairly thick mixture at this stage.

Now add a large tin of Heinz cream of tomato soup and stir well. Warm gently until hot and add a couple of teaspoons of Marmite (or enough to taste) and ground black pepper. Add a tin of drained processed peas and the reserved meat, or any cold turkey you may have left. When the soup is piping hot, serve with Melba toast.

LEFTOVER TURKEY WITH CURRY

2 oz butter
2 medium onions, finely chopped
1 clove of garlic, crushed
2 oz plain flour
1-2 tablespoons curry powder
1 stock cube
½ teaspoon cumin
tin of evaporated milk and approximately 10 fl oz water
salt and pepper to taste
cubed cooked turkey

Melt butter in a large saucepan. Sauté onion and garlic until tender. Blend in flour, curry, cumin, stock cube, seasoning. Gradually stir in evaporated milk and water. Stir until it thickens. Add turkey and cook until heated through. Serve on a bed of rice and with some Roseden chutney.

CURRY SAUCE FOR CHICKEN, MEAT, FISH OR VEGETABLES

Freeze in 1 pint containers, makes approximately 3 pints.

4 oz butter and a tablespoon of olive oil
2 large chopped onions
2 large chopped cooking apples
2 oz plain flour
4 teaspoons curry powder (or use curry paste and curry powder)
2 pints chicken stock
3 tablespoons sweet chutney
2 tablespoons tomato paste
juice of half a lemon
(To vary I sometimes add sultanas and grated rind of an orange)

Melt the butter and oil in a pan and add the onions and apples, cook over a low heat without browning for about 8-10 minutes. Stir in the curry powder and cook for a further 5 minutes, stirring. Add the flour and cook for another minute, still stirring. Add the stock. Bring to the boil. Add the rest of the ingredients. Cook gently for a little les than an hour. Cool quickly. Put in containers and freeze.
When re-heating, break up in the pan and stir with a wooden spoon. Be sure to check the seasoning.

ELIZABETH'S CHICKEN SALAD

1 cold cooked chicken or turkey, cut into pieces
4 hard-boiled eggs
2 celery hearts or green peppers
8 oz green grapes
3 oz salted almonds
French dressing
1 carton plain yoghurt
juice of 1 lemon
1 tablespoon sugar
salt and pepper

Separate yolks from whites of eggs and chop whites. Cut celery into strips, or de-seed, blanch and slice green peppers. De-pip and skin grapes.
Mix all ingredients (including chicken/turkey pieces) in a bowl and toss well in French dressing. Arrange in serving dish and sprinkle with sieved egg yolks, black pepper and nuts.
Mix yoghurt, lemon juice, sugar, salt and pepper to make a sour cream dressing and serve with the salad.

SALMI OF PHEASANT

Enough for 6 depending on amount of meat.

leftover pheasant
2 oz butter
1 oz flour
1 small onion
2 glasses of port
pinch of herbs
1 tablespoon redcurrant jelly
1 pint of stock (made from pheasant bones)
2 bay leaves
salt and freshly ground black pepper

Cut the meat into neat pieces. Melt the butter in a pan and brown the flour. Add the stock, stir until it boils. Add the finely chopped onion, herbs, jelly, wine and bay leaves. Simmer for approximately 20 minutes.
Strain and add pheasant, season and re-heat. Garnish with triangles of fried bread.

***Gift tags** are easily made from last year's Christmas cards. Simply cut out motifs with pinking shears, make a hole in one corner and thread fine ribbon or string through. Make sure the back of the tag is blank for your message.*

GAMMON WITH A CHEESY TOPPING

Good served as a supper dish or for breakfast

gammon rashers, 1 good sized one per person
1½ oz thinly sliced Cheddar cheese for each rasher

Grill gammon and when cooked add cheese and return to grill for about a minute until cheese has melted.
A cored, thinly sliced apple ring can be added when the gammon is cooked, grill this for 2 minutes before adding the cheese.
You could also make this dish using thick slices of cooked ham — simply add cheese and grill.

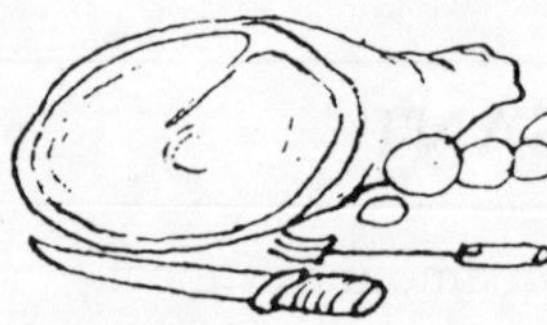

COLD HAM SOUFFLÉ

Use a 2-pint soufflé dish or half mixture for a 1-pint dish. If preferred use ramekins.

1 lb minced cooked ham
2 oz butter
2 oz plain flour
1 pint milk
1 teaspoon chopped tarragon
8 eggs, separated
½ pint single cream
8 level teaspoons gelatine
8 tablespoons water
salt and pepper

Make a white sauce with flour, butter and milk and beat in the egg yolks. Dissolve the gelatine in warm water and add to the sauce. Mix ham and tarragon and add to the sauce with the cream. Season to taste. Whisk egg whites until stiff and fold into the mixture. Put into prepared soufflé dish (tie a collar of paper round the top) and leave to set. Garnish with rolls of sliced ham.

STILTON SOUP

If you've had a whole or half Stilton cheese you may well be left with a hollow shell and a few crumbs at the bottom. Try this delicious soup recipe to use the leftovers.

8 oz Stilton cheese
2 tablespoons butter
1 onion, finely chopped
2 sticks celery, chopped
1½ tablespoons flour
2 pints chicken stock
¼ cup white wine
½ pint milk
3 tablespoons cream
salt and pepper

Fry onions and celery gently in butter until transparent. Stir in flour, add stock, milk and wine and heat, stirring all the time. Simmer for 10 minutes. Stir in the crumbled cheese and season. Simmer for a further 5 minutes, or until the cheese has melted. Whizz in a food processor and return to the pan. Serve hot with a swirl of cream and a sprinkling of chopped chives or parsley.

HAM AND ASPARAGUS QUICHE

4 oz cooked ham, chopped
4-5 oz Cheddar cheese, grated
1 small onion, chopped
2 large eggs
tin of asparagus
½ pint single (or double) cream
knob of butter
5 grinds of black pepper
8 oz shortcrust pastry

Line flan tin with pastry. Beat eggs with cream. Cook onion in butter, add ham and cheese and stir until melted. Remove from heat and cool slightly. Stir in the eggs and cream and season with pepper. Keep tips of asparagus to decorate top and chop remainder, putting in base of flan case. Pour over mixture while still warm. Bake Gas 6/400°F/200°C for approximately 30 minutes until set, but not solid.

FINNAN HADDOCK

1½ lb finnan haddock
1 pint milk
2 oz butter
2 oz flour
2 eggs, hard-boiled

Skin the fish and cut into pieces. Poach in the milk until tender. Drain off the milk and make up to a pint.
Melt the butter, add the flour and cook for a couple of minutes. Blend in the milk.
Flake the fish, making sure there are not any bones left in. Add to the sauce, season. Put on dishes and garnish with wedges of hard-boiled egg.
I do smoked haddock this way leaving it whole, pouring over a little sauce and topping with a poached egg.

SCRAMBLED EGG ON A POTATO CAKE

Shape some leftover mashed potato into flat cakes. Fry in bacon fat slightly browning one side, turn and make a hollow in this side with the back of a spoon. Return to pan and gently brown the base while preparing the scrambled egg. I don't think I need to give a recipe for that! Fill the hollowed out centres with the scrambled egg.

EGGS COCOTTE

Put some chopped bacon into ramekins and bake in the top of the oven Gas 4/350°F/180°C for 7-10 minutes until just cooked. Break an egg into each dish and sprinkle with salt and pepper. Put a dot or two of butter on each egg and bake above the centre of the oven for 7-10 minutes until lightly set.

BREAKFAST PICK-ME-UP

For jaded palates. For each person: juice of 1 orange, a tablespoon of clear honey and 1 egg. Whizz in a food processor or liquidiser and serve.

Preserves and Edible Gifts

I like to receive presents where a lot of thought and love has gone into the making. And I love to give home made presents too. Here are just a few ideas for preserves, which you can make well ahead, and some delicious sweetmeats.

RUM POT

This is a traditional way of preserving summer fruits to eat later in the year; and Christmas is the ideal time to sample the fruits of your labours. Start your rum pot in the summer when cherries and strawberries are plentiful and continue adding diferent fruits in layers as they become available until your pot is full. Your container can be as grand as a proper continental *rumtopf* or as simple as glass preserving jars, or jam jars with lids. For each pound of prepared fruit you will need 8 oz of sugar and rum to cover — you'll need 1-2 bottles of light or dark rum. All fruit should be washed. Stones should be remove from cherries, peaches, plums, apricots, and the larger fruit halved or quartered. Kiwi fruit should be peeled and sliced and seedless grapes are best. Pineapple should be peeled and cut into chunks. Weigh out fruit and lay in a large bowl sprinkling on half its weight of sugar. Leave until the juices run into the sugar — about an hour, then transfer to the jar. Cover with rum and make sure all fruit is immersed. Cover with cling film and lid. Continue adding fruit, with sugar and covering with rum, until the jar or pot is full. Seal with lid and leave for 2 or 3 months. Serve with cream or ice cream or meringues or even all three! You'll only need small portions of rum pot because it is very alcoholic. If you want to give as presents, transfer to attractive jars and label.

If you get hooked on making rum pots you may well end up with a surplus of syrup when all the fruit has been devoured. Strain this syrup into clean bottles and store. It can be used in a variety of ways from adding to fruit cakes, to flame bananas or pineapple, and making babas!

CHERRIES IN BRANDY

As with the rum pot, bottle some sunshine to serve in the depths of winter.

2 lb ripe cherries, washed and stoned
grated rind of an orange
12 blanched almonds
brandy

Pack all ingredients except brandy into clean, wide-necked glass jars (save attractive jars such as continental jam jars, or stoppered glass jars, particularly if planning on giving as presents). Fill to the top with brandy and cover tightly. Store in a cool, dark place for at least a month. Serve with cream or in thin pancakes.

PRUNES IN PORT

ready-to-eat pitted prunes
port

Follow the above recipe for method, packing the prunes into jars and topping up with port. Seal and store until required.

I like to give 'foody' presents to friends. I look for attractive containers which can then be re-used. Flavoured sugar is always welcomed by fellow cooks.

FLAVOURED SUGARS

Vanilla sugar
1 lb sugar, caster or granulated
vanilla pod

Cover vanilla pod with sugar and seal the jar. Wait for a couple of weeks before using.

Citrus sugar
grated rind of lemon and orange
1 lb sugar

Dry the grated rind in a low oven. Cool and add to the sugar. Seal the container, and don't forget to add a label.

Spicy sugar
1 lb sugar
1 cinnamon stick
3 cloves

Put spices into container with sugar, seal and store as before.

MISS MILVAIN'S RUNNER BEAN CHUTNEY

2 lb runner beans (after trimming)
1½ lb peeled chopped onions
1 lb demerara sugar
1 lb soft brown sugar
1 heaped tablespoon cornflour
1 tablespoon turmeric
1 tablespoon dry mustard
1½ pints vinegar

Cook the sliced beans in salted water until tender. Cook onions in ½ pint of vinegar until soft. Mix dry ingredients (not the sugar) to a smooth paste with a little vinegar. Add the rest of the vinegar and cook for 10 minutes. Add the sugar and strained beans together with the onions and boil for 15 minutes. Pot in the usual way and cover and label.

CONSERVED CRANBERRIES

This is a dual-purpose preserve, although its shelf-life is limited.

1 lb cranberries
8 oz granulated sugar
1 large orange, grated rind and juice

Wash and dry the berries and place in a bowl with the sugar and orange rind and juice. Now here's another case where your hands come in handy. Mix with your hands until the sugar has dissolved. Pack into clean hot jars and seal in the usual way. Store in the fridge for 3-4 weeks. Stir before using either with turkey, chicken or ham, or as a dessert with whipped cream.

Sweets make ideal gifts, particularly if you want to involve the younger members of the family in making their own presents for Granny or Grandad. An easy one to start with is to use marzipan left over from icing the cake.

MARZIPAN PETIT FRUITS

scraps of leftover marzipan
food colouring
cloves

Colour the marzipan in different colours according to the fruit being made — yellow for bananas, orange for oranges, green and red for apples, purple for bunches of grapes. Mould into small fruit shapes. Press oranges on the fine grater for the orange-peel look and use cloves for stalks. Paint brown lines on the 'bananas', paint red patches on to the green 'apples' and use a clove for a stalk. You'll soon get the hang of it. Put each fruit into a small paper sweet case and arrange in a small box or basket. Cover with cling film, add a pretty bow and keep till the DAY in a cool place.

PEPPERMINT CREAMS

leftover fondant or royal icing
peppermint flavouring
icing sugar

Flavour the icing with peppermint and stiffen if necessary with extra icing sugar. You need a consistency that you can roll out with a rolling pin. Colour some green if liked. Roll out to ⅛″ thick and cut into small rounds. Put into paper sweet cases and keep cool until required.

YUMMY RUM TRUFFLES

This is a recipe for a fairly large quantity.
7 oz good dark chocolate
4 oz butter
4 tablespoons rum
4 egg yolks
4 oz ground almonds
12 oz icing sugar

Melt chocolate and butter. Stir in rum and egg yolks. Add ground almonds and sieved icing sugar. Mix well and put in fridge to firm.
Shape into small balls. Roll in dark chocolate vermicelli.
(Arranged in small paper cases and put in a fancy box they make a good present for the person who has everything!)

MARY'S CHOCOLATE SPECIALS

4 oz butter
4 oz chopped nuts
4 oz glacé cherries
8 oz icing sugar
6 oz dessicated coconut
2 teaspoons coffee essence (or Camp coffee)
10 oz good plain chocolate, melted

Cream the butter and sugar and mix in the nuts, chopped cherries, coconut and coffee essence. Roll into small balls and, using a fork, dip each one into melted chocolate. Decorate each sweet with half a cherry. Keep cool until required.

ROSEDEN FUDGE

1 lb granulated sugar
5 fl oz evaporated milk (small tin)
4 oz margarine
pinch cream of tartar
few drops vanilla essence

Put all the ingredients into a large saucepan and bring to the boil, stirring occasionally. Boil for about 15 minutes or until it reaches the soft ball stage (test in a cup of cold water — if it can be formed into a soft ball with the fingers it is ready). Remove from the heat and beat for 5 minutes. Pour into a baking tray and mark into squares.

The Language of Flowers from Days Gone By

Rosemary for remembrance
Pansies for thoughts
Mint for suspicion and lavender distrust.
(A red rosebud, an unspoken proposal from a young man, a white rosebud in return for acceptance!

LAVENDER BAGS

Gather sprigs of lavender from the garden in the summer when the weather is dry. Hang in a warm place until the small flowers are dry. Strip the flowers from the stems and use to fill small bags made from scraps of cotton. Tie with pretty ribbon. Can be used to scent linen and clothes and make nice gifts. Throw the stems on the fire to give a lovely aroma!

POT-POURRI

Gather rose petals on a dry day in summer, dry in a warm, dark place. Collect other scented leaves such as scented geranium, mint, rosemary and thyme and dry in the same way. Dry orange and lemon peel and grind to a powder. Mix all together with spices such as cloves or cinnamon, if liked. Pack into attractive containers, or open baskets or bowls. Use to scent rooms. Make small cotton bags and fill to scent clothes.

Handy hint

I've worked out a good way of lining loaf tins with greaseproof or baking parchment. Simply place your tin on the parchment and draw round its base. Measure the depth of the tin and add this measurement all round to give you a larger rectangle.

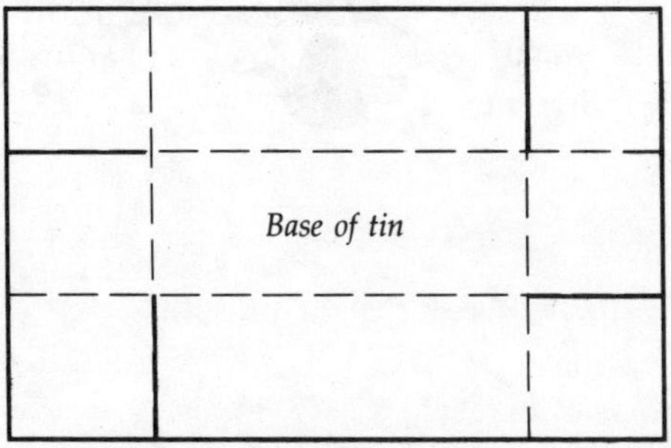

Fold along broken lines, cut along solid lines. Place in tin and fold flaps round to give a neat lining.

Drinks

Just a few country recipes here for warming drinks plus some ideas for wine at Christmas.

TIA MARIA

This recipe came from Joy in Canada

(1 cup = 8 oz)

2½ cups dark brown sugar
1 tablespoon vanilla
1½ cups water
3 heaped tablespoons instant coffee

Mix all ingredients and bring to the boil. Cool. Add 25 oz bottle alcohol. Pour into bottles and keep in a cool place.
Canadian alcohol is white and does not have any flavour. If not obtainable here Joy suggests a South African brandy or vodka.

ORANGE WINE

1 bottle dry white wine
1 lemon, grated rind only
2 oranges, grated rind only
1 vanilla pod
½ cinnamon stick

Combine all the ingredients in a bottle, cap and shake. Store in a cool dark place for about two weeks. Strain and serve as an aperitif.

EGG NOG

1 egg white (free range)
1 tablespoon brandy
1 tablespoon cream
caster sugar

Whisk the egg white. Mix together the brandy, cream and sugar to taste and stir in the egg white. Serve immediately.

BLACKBERRY GIN

1 lb blackberries
4 oz sugar
16 fl oz gin

You need a pound of the ripest, juciest berries you can find. Crush them slightly and put into a jar, adding the sugar and the gin. Screw on the lid tightly and leave for 3 months, shaking regularly for the first few weeks. Strain into bottles and seal. Label with attractive labels.

SLOE GIN

This is another good country recipe which proves very warming on a cold day. Finding the sloes is usually the problem here, but if you know where to look. . . .

1 lb sloes
¾ lb sugar
1 bottle gin

Prick each sloe all over with a large needle. Place in a screw top jar or wide-mouthed bottle and add sugar and gin. Seal the bottle or jar and leave for 3 months shaking occasionally. Strain into a new bottle and label.

MULLED WINE

For approximately 25 glasses you will need at least 3 bottles of red wine, a half bottle of port and about 10 tablespoons of rum.
Take about 6 oz light muscavado sugar and dissolve in 10 fl oz water in a large pan. Slice the rind of a lemon and a couple of oranges thinly (I use a potato peeler). Put about 7 cloves into another orange and add all to the pan with a stick of cinnamon. Infuse gently for 10 to 15 minutes. Add wine, port and rum and bring almost to the boil. Remove from heat. Put into warmed heat-proof jugs and pour into glasses.

MULLED WINE (WITHOUT THE WINE!)

1 carton apple juice
1 carton red grape juice
2 oranges, quartered
8 cloves
1 cinnamon stick
honey

Stick a clove into each orange quarter and put in a large saucepan. Pour on the apple juice and grape juice and a tablespoon of honey. Add the cinnamon stick and heat gently for about 10 minutes. Serve hot in heatproof glasses. This is delicious on a cold day with mince pies.

LEMON BARLEY WATER

Wash half a pint of pearl barley in warm water. Add 4 pints of boiling water and let it stand for 8 or 9 hours.
Peel 3 lemons very finely and boil the peel with 4 oz of caster sugar in 1½ pints of boiling water.
Strain the barley into one dish and strain the peel into the same dish and add the juice of 9 lemons.

SOME IDEAS FOR WINE AT CHRISTMAS

by Graham McHarg of Irvine Robertson Wines

Christmas is a time for festivities, so why not start off with a bottle of champagne — yes even for breakfast! There are plenty of champagnes around at £10 to £11 per bottle these days, and if you think far enough ahead, and buy some in mid-summer, put it away on its side in a cool dark place until Christmas, you will be rewarded for your foresight — even the youngest and sharpest wines will improve almost beyond belief over six to nine months. If you get tired of champagne, try one of the ever improving Sauvignon Blancs from South Africa or New Zealand! Gewurztraminer from Alsace in France also works well, and is not quite so dry.

With the roast, be it turkey, pork or goose, the important thing is to drink what you really like — virtually every wine made could accompany these roasts without causing an upset. Amongst the white wines (good if you want to be awake for the Queen's speech), a good Chablis — or any of the wines I suggested for the starter would make admirable partners — the acidity cutting through the richness of pork or goose, and the fruit and balance complementing the turkey. For red wines, my personal choice would be as fine a bottle of red Burgundy as you can persuade the bank manager to finance — in an ideal world a 1978 or 1985 (in Heaven a 1947 or 1959!) vintage of at least premier cru quality, from a traditional style grower — or why not be different and try Château Musar from Lebanon — but beware, you may get hooked on it!

Moving on to the Christmas pudding and mince pies, there is a lot to be said for not changing a winning combination — a fine Cognac or Armagnac would go down a treat. A rich old Oloroso sherry if you can find one, or one of the rich southerly Muscats such as Beaumes de Venise or even very well chilled Asti Spumante would all go splendidly.

If you have room for cheese, port and Stilton is a wonderful tradition but please never pour the port over or into the cheese. It does nothing at all for the cheese. Most English blue cheeses, and the stronger flavoured hard cheeses will partner port very well, and it is always worth looking around at this time of year for offers of aged tawny ports, or late bottled vintages. If you can't finish the bottle on Christmas day most will keep till old year's night and still give much pleasure. If you are serving mild cheeses or creamy ones like Brie, a good bottle of claret would be wonderful; if you have the stamina — or even finish up any of the white wines we started with — you will not be disappointed with the way they partner the cheese. So there we are, back to square one . . . if there is any of that champagne left, the washer-up would like a glass!

INDEX

IRVINE ROBERTSON WINES

Graham MacHarg

Fine Wines

Irvine Robertson Wines Limited, 10/11 North Leith Sands, Edinburgh EH6 4ER
Telephone: 031-553 3521 · Facsimile: 031-553 5465
Wooler Office: Fowberry Tower, Wooler, Northumberland NE71 6ER.
Telephone: 06685 274 · Facsimile: 06685 442

We supply many highly regarded hotels and restaurants in Northumberland, the Borders, the Lake District and throughout Scotland — can we supply you?

We also have an efficient local delivery service, mail order service nationwide and an interesting descriptive list of some 300 wines at very competitive prices. If you would like a copy please telepone or send me your name and address.

GRAHAM MacHARG
Fowberry Tower, Wooler, Northumberland NE71 6ER
Telephone: 06685 274 · Fax: 06685 442

WOODSIDE RECLAMATION

Architectural Antiques · Traditional Building Materials

Visit our yard and shop for a wide selection of original fixtures and fittings. Whether you are restoring an old house or building a new one or just want to add character to your home with the odd item of architectural interest, we have plenty to tempt you.
Always in stock: Georgian, Victorian and Edwardian fireplaces, cast-iron baths and other bathroom fittings, radiators, panel doors, brassware, traditional building materials as well as numerous other architectural items. We also offer a stripping and restoration and cleaning service for customers' own fittings.
You'll find us at Woodside in Scremerston and also at the village shop in Scremerston. Woodside Reclamtion is on the A1 just south of Berwick-upon-Tweed. Open 9-5 Monday to Saturday. Telephone 0289 331211/303582/302658